App Development Guide: Wack-A Mole

Learn App Develop By Creating Apps for iOS,
Android and the Web

By
Mark Lassoff
with Chris Coscina

LearnToProgram Media

Vernon, Connecticut

LearnToProgram.tv, Incorporated
27 Hartford Turnpike Suite 206
Vernon, CT 06066

contact@learntoprogram.tv

(860) 840-7090

ISBN-13: 978-0692607732 (LearnToProgram, Incorporated)
ISBN-10: 0692607730

About the App Development Guide series

The App Development Guide series from LearnToProgram Media is designed to provide you with guides to creating interesting apps. The app development guides provide all of the code, assets, and other materials you will need to create complete applications. Some apps in this series are designed to work within a web browser—others are designed to be deployed to mobile devices—either as a native iOS or Android App or as a HTML5 based app that works on both platforms.

I think that, naturally, the best way to learn app development is to actually build apps. Our goal is not to provide an exhaustive explanation for every tag, method and property we use in building the apps. In this series, it is our hope that the guides will provide context to integrate what you've learned previously, and, perhaps, set you up for future learning.

I hope you gain a great deal of satisfaction from coding along with these guides and making the app work on your own. Once you've got the app working I'd invite you to modify the app—add features and make it more interesting, usable or useful.

I am a big believer in the learn-by-doing paradigm—It's how I gained much of the skillset I boast today. I hope after working through our App Development Guide series that you will feel the same.

If you have any feedback about any of the books in this series, please don't hesitate to reach out to me at mark@learntoprogram.tv or @mlassoff on Twitter.

Technologies

This app development guide uses the following technologies:

• HTML5
• Javascript
• CSS (Cascading Style Sheets)

The final application may be fun on any contemporary Mac or PC with current browser.

Assets and Code

All of the assets and code for this book are available to you at https://learntoprogram.tv/pages/request-book-assets. Simply provide your email address as directed and you will receive a linke to the assets and code via email in just a few minutes.

Table of Contents

Introduction

We will be diving deep into creating our own game from scratch. It will be just like the Wack-A-Mole games that you may remember from Dave & Busters or Discovery Zone; truly a classic favorite. Instead of using a mallet to wack the moles, we will be using mouse clicks (or touches on a touchscreen). It uses only HTML5, CSS, and Javascript. We will also make liberal use of **CreateJS**. *CreateJS* is a whole entire world of Javascript libraries and tools designed to enhance a user's web experience with animation, sound, and interactivity. You will need at least a rudimentary knowledge of HTML, CSS, and Javascript to keep pace with this material. However, you won't need any foreknowledge of *CreateJS*, and links will be provided to documentation on the specific libraries and classes that we use in our game.

Playing the Game

Before we analyze all of the code that makes our game do what it does, we should first understand what our game does and how it works from an external perspective. By external perspective, I mean the perspective of a user playing the game. The internal perspective is of the programmer reading or writing the code that makes everything work. As programmers, our ultimate goal is to understand and manifest the internal (under the hood) workings of entities, processes, and systems via code (which is essentially just communication, as all programming is written in some sort of language). However, understanding the external side of things, such as objects in the real world that you're trying to model, is foundational to being able to implement them internally through the art of coding.

Just in case you've never played the real-world version of Wack A Mole, I'll summarize the general idea of it. The objective is simple – to wack as many moles as possible using a hand-held mallet. These little moles (which are basically just stuffed animals, but more sturdy) pop out of little holes on a table in front of you. Your goal is to hit the moles with your mallet, which causes them to go back down into their hole. Each mole only stays out of the hole for a short period of time, and if you miss your chance to wack it, then you miss the points you would receive for wacking it. Earning more points usually means winning extra tickets to buy prizes, so there is an incentive to wack the moles. Some players even cheat by laying the arms of two people over the holes; constantly covering the holes so that the moles are considered wacked as soon as they begin to pop out. Be careful using this technique, as it could get you kicked out of Dave & Busters (or wherever else you may try it out).

The context of our Wack A mole app is really not much different than the original version. The main difference is that instead of using a physical mallet, we use a mouse or our fingers. Also, the moles are not physical objects, but instead are just images on a computer screen. This takes away from some of the fun, but it does make it much more convenient – since it's accessible virtually anywhere via a computer or phone.

The game first begins by showing a title screen (as shown in Figure 2-1) and playing background music.

Figure 2-1 – The Main Title Screen

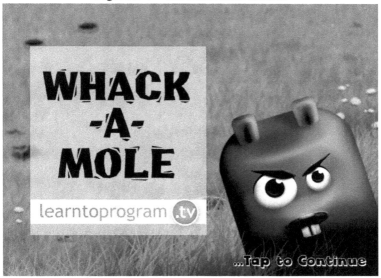

Each level also has a title screen. Once the game begins, the music changes and the moles begin popping out of their holes. The moles taunt you and laugh at you. When you click on them (or tap via touchscreen), then they go back down into their holes. For every mole you wack, you earn more points. Finally, there is a limited number of time in each level, and the levels increase in difficulty as you progress (as moles come out of their holes more frequently in higher levels). It's essentially just a software version of the physical game. There are only three levels, and after completing the third level you are presented with a Game Over screen (as shown in Figure 2-2). You may choose to play again (starting at level one) simply by clicking/tapping the Game Over screen. If you haven't already, play this game through to completion at least a few times to get a general feel for it.

Figure 2-2: The Game Over Screen

Assets – Images, Animations, and Sounds

Now that we have become familiar with the game itself, let's take a look at the various components. The code of our game is a "hidden" component in the sense that we don't see it, and it's a bit more esoteric in nature than the other components. Besides the code, our game primarily consists of images, sounds, and sprite animations. Let's take a look at these assets (the images, sounds and animations), which are present in the Assets folder.

The Assets folder contains four other folders: backgroundTiles, loadingScreens, sounds, and spriteAnimations. These should all be relatively self-explanatory, but actually go into each folder and open up some of the files. Our backgroundTiles folder contains PNG files that are used for the various "tiles" of our game. The game board is broke up into an x and y grid, with a tile at each coordinate. The tile for a hole (which a mole may pop out of) is shown in Figure 3-1, and the tile for plain grass (with nothing on top of it) is shown in Figure 3-2:

Figure 3-1: The Hole Tile (Assets/backgroundTiles/bt_hole.png)

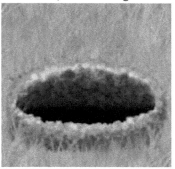

Figure 3-2: The Grass Tile (Assets/backgroundTiles/bt_grass.png)

The loadingScreens folder contains JPG files which are used for the various loading screens. For example, the loading screen when you initially start the game is the image shown in Figure 3-3, and the loading screen for level two is the image shown in Figure 3-4:

Figure 3-3: Title Screen (Assets/loadingScreens/ls_title.jpg)

Figure 3-4: Level Two Loading Screen
(Assets/loadingScreens/ls_level2.jpg)

Our sounds folder contains the various sounds used in our game. For example, welcome.mp3 is the sound played when we welcome the player with the title screen. This is also the sound played in the Game Over screen. The laugh.mp3 file is played when a mole laughs at you, the hit.mp3 file is played when you hit a mole, and the circus1.mp3, circus2.mp3, and circus3.mp3 files are used as the background music of each levels (circus1 is used for level one, circus2 is used for level two, and circus 3 is used for level three).

The items contained in the spriteAnimations folder are a bit more complicated than the other folders. A **sprite sheet** is used for what is known as a sprite animation. Sprite animations are made up of multiple images, each image representing a frame of the animation. However, to put all of the images of an animation into separate files would take a lot of time when loading and rendering the images. Therefore, a *sprite sheet* is used to put several images into one image file, and each frame is represented by only a fraction of that image file. For example, let's look at the spritesheet_pop.png file in Figure 3-5:

Figure 3-5: Pop Sprite Sheet
(Assets/spriteAnimations/spritesheet_pop.png)

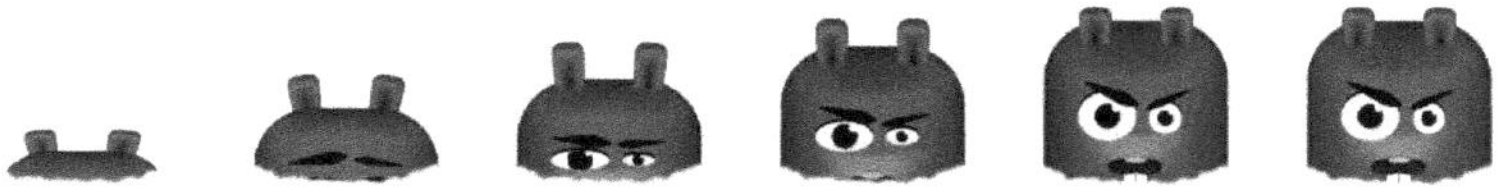

This *sprite sheet* is used for the animation played when a mole pops out of a hole. As you can see, although it's only one image file, it's used as though it is six different images, with each image representing a frame of the animation. If you go into the Pop Up And Down Frames folder, you will also find two other files – a css file and a txt file. The css and txt file contain information about the height, width, and position of each frame in the animation. Open up these files and take a look at them to gain an understanding of how our application uses our *sprite sheets*.

Now that we have played the game and have become familiar with the game assets, let's begin understanding the source code of our game. We will cover each source code file one by one, since there are many source code files in our application.

The Container - index.html and mole.css

Our index.html file and mole.css file are both quite minimal. The reason being is that we aren't primarily using HTML or CSS for our game, the source code of our game is primarily made up of Javascript. Let's take a look at the source code of index.html and mole.css, so that we may break them down piece by piece:

Code Listing 4-1: index.html

```
<html>
    <head>
        <meta charset="utf-8" />
        <meta name="format-detection"
content="telephone=no" />
        <meta name="msapplication-tap-highlight"
content="no" />
        <!-- WARNING: for iOS 7, remove the width=device-
width and height=device-height attributes. See
https://issues.apache.org/jira/browse/CB-4323 -->
        <meta name="viewport" content="user-scalable=no,
initial-scale=1, maximum-scale=1, minimum-scale=1,
width=device-width, height=device-height, target-
densitydpi=device-dpi" />
        <script type="text/javascript"
src="createjs.js"></script>
        <script type="text/javascript"
src="constants.js"></script>
        <script type="text/javascript"
src="globals.js"></script>
        <script type="text/javascript"
src="game.js"></script>
```

```
        <script type="text/javascript"
src="display.js"></script>
        <link href="mole.css" rel="stylesheet" />
        <title>Whack-a-Mole</title>
    </head>
    <body>
        <canvas id="myCanvas"></canvas>
    </body>
</html>
```

Code Listing 4-2: mole.css

```
body
{
    margin: 0px;
}

#myCanvas
{
    background-color: green;
}
```

One of the first thing's you may notice in index.html is the various **meta** tags. The *meta* elements are used to contain information about the HTML document, or configure settings for the document. Here are brief descriptions of how we use each *meta* tag:

The *meta* tag named format-detection is used to turn off detection of telephone numbers by setting the content attribute of the tag to "telephone=no". This prevents 10 or 11 digit numbers from turning into links (since phone numbers are 10 and 11 digits, some devices display them as links by default). Your score probably won't get that high anyway, but we've prevented that problem it just in case.

- The *meta* tag named misapplication-tap-highlight is used to turn off tap highlighting on Windows devices.
- The *meta* tag named viewport configures various settings for our viewport.

Next, you'll notice various <script> tags that reference the various Javascript files used by our application. These files are really what do most of the work in our game. We also link to the CSS style sheet named mole.css. Our style sheet is extremely simple – all it does is set the margin of our document to zero, and sets the background color of our **canvas** element (named myCanvas) to green.

The body of our index.html document only contains one element – the *canvas* element. The HTML *canvas* element is used as a container for rendering graphics. Therefore, all our index.html file does is render our game in a web browser via that *canvas* element. In our case, we will be displaying all of our asset files on our *canvas* via the code in our Javascript files. In other words, it's essentially just used as a container for our game – all of the actual processing and logic happens elsewhere.

CreateJS – createjs.js

I mentioned earlier that *CreateJS* is a set of libraries and tools for adding sound, graphics, animation, and interactivity to our game. We won't be looking at the source code for *CreateJS* (which is located in the createjs.js file), since we don't really need to know the inner workings of the libraries, we just need to use their interfaces. Some links will be provided to official documentation of different APIs and components that we use from *CreateJS* as we come across them. The

CreateJS documentation is a great place in general to explore all of the different possibilities that you have with it. Our game only explores a small fraction of everything that *CreateJS* has to offer.

CreateJS consists of smaller libraries such as **EaselJS**, **TweenJS**, **SoundJS** and **PreloadJS**. Let's go take a look at a quick overview of each:

EaselJS is primarily used for creating and rendering graphics, text, and animations via the HTML5 *canvas* element (which we saw earlier in our index.html). For more information on *EaselJS*, check out the official documentation at: http://www.createjs.com/docs/easeljs/modules/EaselJS.html

- *TweenJS* is designed for tweening animation. I'm sure you may be confused by the word tweening (as I certainly was). Tweening is defined as generating the values between two points. For example, the points between (1, 2) and (4, 5) is (2,3) and (3, 4) if following a straight line (but keep in mind that not all lines/trajectories are necessarily straight). *TweenJS* has great synergy with *EaselJS*, since it can add neat features to your animations. For more information on *TweenJS*, check out the official documentation at: http://www.createjs.com/docs/tweenjs/modules/TweenJS.html

- *SoundJS* is an API for working with sound. It's used to create sounds, play/pause/stop sounds, change the volume of sounds, load sounds, and even install plugins. For more information on *SoundJS*, check out the official documentation at: http://www.createjs.com/docs/soundjs/modules/SoundJS.ht ml

- *PreloadJS* is used for preloading our assets. Preloading refers to the initial loading that takes place before the rest of our application executes. For more information on PreloadJS, check out the official documentation at: http://www.createjs.com/docs/preloadjs/modules/PreloadJS .html

Although you could use any of the above libraries by themselves, they're all included in *CreateJS* – so we only need to reference our createjs.js file. I obtained my *CreateJS* file from the following URL:

https://code.createjs.com/createjs-2015.05.21.min.js

I changed the file name by removing the date and .min, so the file name has been simplified to createjs.js. This Javascript file is then referenced in our index.html code by the following line:

```
<script type="text/javascript" src="createjs.js"></script>
```

That's really all we have to do to install *CreateJS*.
Alternatively, we could also simply reference the URL that
we got the file from, but this would require us to have an
active internet connection to play the game. An example
referencing the URL is as follows:

```
<script src="https://code.createjs.com/createjs-
2015.05.21.min.js"></script>
```

Keep in mind that the exact URL may change, since the
date of the most recent version is a part of the URL. The
latest version should generally be available on
createjs.com.

Helper Files – constants.js, display.js, and globals.js

The bulk of the source code for our game is in the game.js file, but
there are a few Javascript files that we use as helpers for specific
things. They might not make complete sense to you right now, but as
you see how they are used within game.js, you will become more
familiar with their purpose and meaning. Let's take a look at each,
starting with constants.js:

Code Listing 6-1: constants.js

```
var constant = new Object();
constant.WIDTH=1024;
constant.HEIGHT=768;
constant.TILEWIDTH= 170;
constant.TILEHEIGHT= 168;
```

```
constant.COLUMNS = 6;
constant.ROWS = 5;
constant.LEVEL1FREQUENCY = 33;
constant.LEVEL2FREQUENCY = 26;
constant.LEVEL3FREQUENCY = 19;
constant.LEVELTIME = 20;
```

As the name of the file implies, constants.js is used to store the various constant values used by our application. A constant value is a value that's never supposed to change. It's useful to put all of our constants into one place, so that way it's not difficult to find where each of our constant values are defined. If we needed to search through our various source code files to find where a particular constant is defined, that would waste a lot of time.

We first create an object named constant, and then we set various properties of our constant object. Each property represents something different. The WIDTH and HEIGHT properties represent the height and width of our *canvas* in the index.html file. The TILEHEIGHT and TILEWIDTH properties contain the values for the width and height of the game tiles. As mentioned earlier, our *canvas* is made up of an x and y grid of tiles. The COLUMNS and ROWS properties define the number of columns and rows in that grid. The LEVEL1FREQUENCY, LEVEL2FREQUENCY, and LEVEL3FREQUENCY are used in calculations that determine the frequency at which our moles pop out of the holes. A lower number causes the moles to come out of their holes more frequently (by coming out of the holes more frequently, the game becomes more difficult). The LEVELTIME property specifies the amount of seconds allocated to each level – which means that each level lasts for twenty seconds. You can experiment with changing some of the values to see how they change the game. For example, you could change the level time from 20 to 10 or 30. You could also adjust the frequency of each level to make the game easier or more difficult.

Now let's take a look at display.js:

Code Listing 6-2: display.js

```
var display = new Object();
display.stage = null;
display.queue = null;
display.hitAnimation = null;
display.idleAnimation = null;
display.laughingAnimation = null;
display.popAnimation = null;
display.teaseAnimation = null;
```

The general structure of display.js is similar to the structure of constants.js. First, we create an object named display, and then set various properties of that object (which are used in game.js). Each of these properties relate to the visual aspect of our game. The stage property represents the "stage" of our game where everything is displayed. Our stage works directly with our HTML *canvas* element, as everything is displayed in our *canvas*. The queue property is used to store all of our assets. The various animation properties are used to hold each of our sprite animations.

Finally, let's take a look at the globals.js file:

Code Listing 6-3: globals.js

```
var globals = new Object();
globals.level = 1;
globals.playing = false;
globals.gameTime = 0;
```

```
globals.holePositions= null;
globals.score = 0;
globals.scoreText = null;
```

The globals.js file also has the same general structure as constants.js
and display.js. First we create an object named globals, and then set the
various properties of that object. Global variables are variables that are
used throughout your entire program. The values in constants.js and
display.js are also global, but the values in globals.js are other global
values that don't really fit within the other two files (since the
properties here are not constant, and they also don't directly relate to
the visual display of our game).

The level property keeps track of the current level that we are on. Since
we begin at level one, we initialize this value to one. The playing
property keeps track of whether we are actively playing the game. At
the beginning of each level, this value is set to true, and then it is set
back to false at the end of each level. The gameTime represents the
clock of our game. It's reset to zero at the beginning of each level, and
increases by one as each second passes. The holePositions property
keeps track of the x and y values for each hole (the holes that the moles
pop out of). The score keeps track of our score, and the scoreText
property is used for displaying that score.

The Game Logic – game.js

All of our actual game logic is stored in our game.js file, and game.js is
without a doubt the most intricate of all of the Javascript files in our
game (besides createjs.js, but we aren't going to examine the source
code of that file). Due to the complexity of this file, we're actually
going to break it down into several sections, with each section covering

only one to a few functions. Our general approach will be to follow the flow of execution of the program. We will start in the window.onload function, and then examine each function in the order that they are used by the game. This way, you can see how the game processing works step-by-step.

Here is the complete code listing of game.js, although we will display each function again as we examine it in detail:

Code Listing 7-1: game.js

```
//Loads when screen is drawn
//
//
window.onload=function()
{
    init();
    //document.addEventListener('deviceready', init,
false);
}

function init()
{
    setupCanvas();
    preloadAssets();
}

function setupCanvas()
{
    display.stage = new createjs.Stage("myCanvas");
    display.stage.canvas.width = constant.WIDTH;
    display.stage.canvas.height = constant.HEIGHT;
}

function preloadAssets()
{
```

```
    display.queue = new createjs.LoadQueue();
    display.queue.installPlugin(createjs.Sound);
    display.queue.on("complete" , assetsLoaded, this);
    display.queue.loadManifest([
        {id: "ls_title",
src:"assets/loadingScreens/ls_title.jpg"},
        {id: "ls_credit",
src:"assets/loadingScreens/ls_credit.jpg"},
        {id: "ls_gameOver",
src:"assets/loadingScreens/ls_gameOver.jpg"},
        {id: "ls_level1",
src:"assets/loadingScreens/ls_level1.jpg"},
        {id: "ls_level2",
src:"assets/loadingScreens/ls_level2.jpg"},
        {id: "ls_level3",
src:"assets/loadingScreens/ls_level3.jpg"},
        {id: "ls_winner",
src:"assets/loadingScreens/ls_winner.jpg"},
        {id: "bt_grass",
src:"assets/backgroundTiles/bt_grass.png"},
        {id: "bt_hole",
src:"assets/backgroundTiles/bt_hole.png"},
        {id: "bt_flowerRock",
src:"assets/backgroundTiles/bt_flowerRock.png"},
        {id: "bt_rock",
src:"assets/backgroundTiles/bt_rock.png"},
        {id: "bt_flowers",
src:"assets/backgroundTiles/bt_flowers.png"},
        {id: "snd_welcome",
src:"assets/sounds/welcome.mp3"},
        {id: "snd_punch", src:"assets/sounds/punch.mp3"},
        {id: "snd_level1Background",
src:"assets/sounds/circus1.mp3"},
        {id: "snd_level2Background",
src:"assets/sounds/circus2.mp3"},
        {id: "snd_level3Background",
src:"assets/sounds/circus3.mp3"},
        {id: "snd_laugh", src:"assets/sounds/laugh.mp3"},
        {id: "ss_hit",
src:"assets/spriteAnimations/spritesheet_hit.png"},
```

```
        {id: "ss_idle",
src:"assets/spriteAnimations/spritesheet_idle.png"},
        {id: "ss_laughing",
src:"assets/spriteAnimations/spritesheet_laughing.png"},
        {id: "ss_pop",
src:"assets/spriteAnimations/spritesheet_pop.png"},
        {id: "ss_tease",
src:"assets/spriteAnimations/spritesheet_tease.png"}

    ]);
}

function assetsLoaded()
{
    //Display the Level1 Screen
    var background = display.queue.getResult("ls_title");
    display.stage.addChild(new
createjs.Bitmap(background));
    display.stage.update();

    //Reister Sprite Sheets
    registerSpriteSheets();

    //click to start the game
    display.stage.addEventListener("click", function(event)
{ loadLevel(); })

    //Play welcome music
    createjs.Sound.play("snd_welcome");
}

function registerSpriteSheets()
{
    //Hit Spritesheet
    var data = {
        images: [display.queue.getResult("ss_hit")],
        frames: {width:170, height: 168},
        animations: { hit: [0,6] } , framerate: 10
    };
```

```
    var hitSpriteSheet = new createjs.SpriteSheet(data);
    display.hitAnimation = new
createjs.Sprite(hitSpriteSheet, "hit");

    //Idle Spritesheet
    var data = {
        images: [display.queue.getResult("ss_idle")],
        frames: {width:170, height: 168},
        animations: { idle: [0,6] } , framerate: 10
    };

    var idleSpriteSheet = new createjs.SpriteSheet(data);
    display.idleAnimation = new
createjs.Sprite(idleSpriteSheet, "idle");

    //Laughing Spritesheet
    var data = {
        images: [display.queue.getResult("ss_laughing")],
        frames: {width:170, height: 168},
        animations: { laugh: [0,12] } , framerate: 10
    };

    var laughingSpriteSheet = new
createjs.SpriteSheet(data);
    display.laughingAnimation = new
createjs.Sprite(laughingSpriteSheet, "laugh");

    //Pop Animation
    var data = {
        images: [display.queue.getResult("ss_pop")],
        frames: {width:170, height: 168},
        animations: { pop: [0,5] } , framerate: 10
    };

    var popSpriteSheet = new createjs.SpriteSheet(data);
    display.popAnimation = new
createjs.Sprite(popSpriteSheet, "pop");

    //Tease Animation
    var data = {
```

```
        images: [display.queue.getResult("ss_tease")],
        frames: {width:170, height: 168},
        animations: { tease: [0,13] } , framerate: 10
    };

    var teaseSpriteSheet = new createjs.SpriteSheet(data);
    display.teaseAnimation = new
createjs.Sprite(teaseSpriteSheet, "tease");

}

function loadLevel()
{
    //Stop Sounds
    createjs.Sound.stop();

    //Remove Current Click Listener
    display.stage.removeAllEventListeners();

    //Display Level Screen
    display.stage.removeAllChildren();
    display.stage.update();
    var levelLabel = "ls_level" + globals.level;
    var level_screen = display.queue.getResult(levelLabel);
    display.stage.addChild(new
createjs.Bitmap(level_screen));
    display.stage.update();

    //Play Level Music
    var music = "snd_level" + globals.level + "Background";
    createjs.Sound.play(music,{loop:8});

    //Wait for click to start play
    display.stage.addEventListener("click", function(event)
{ startLevel(); })

}

function startLevel()
{
```

```javascript
    //Remove Level Screen
    display.stage.removeAllChildren();
    display.stage.removeAllEventListeners();

    //Display the Level Grid
    var levelGrid = createLevelGrid(constant.COLUMNS,
constant.ROWS);
    displayLevelGrid(levelGrid, constant.COLUMNS,
constant.ROWS);

    //Make a simple array of hole positions
    globals.holePositions = new Array();
    for(x=0; x < levelGrid.length; x++)
    {
        for(y=0; y < levelGrid[x].length; y++)
        {
            if(levelGrid[x][y] == "bt_hole")
            {
                globals.holePositions.push(x);
                globals.holePositions.push(y);
            }
        }
    }

    //start ticker
    createjs.Ticker.setFPS(15);
    createjs.Ticker.addEventListener('tick',
display.stage);
    createjs.Ticker.addEventListener('tick', playLoop);

    playGame();
}

function createLevelGrid(colsNumber, rowsNumber)
{
    var levelGrid= new Array();

    //Each Row
    for(var x=0; x < rowsNumber; x++)
        {
```

```
            var row = new Array();
            //Each column in that row
            for(var y = 0; y < colsNumber; y++)
             {
                 var tileType = Math.floor((Math.random() *
4) + 0);

                 //Associate Graphic with numerical tileType
                 if(tileType ==0)
                 {
                     tileType = "bt_grass";
                 } else if (tileType ==1)
                 {
                     tileType = "bt_hole";
                 } else if (tileType ==2)
                 {
                     tileType = "bt_flowerRock";
                 } else if (tileType ==3)
                 {
                     tileType = "bt_rock";
                 } else
                 {
                     tileType = "bt_flowers";
                 }
                 row[y] = tileType;
             }
             levelGrid[x] = row;
        }
    return levelGrid;
}

function displayLevelGrid(levelGrid, colsNumber,
rowsNumber)
{
    //Where will the tile be positioned?
    var xPos=0;
    var yPos=0;

    for(var x = 0; x < rowsNumber; x++)
    {
```

```
        xPos = 0;
        for(var y =0; y < colsNumber; y++)
        {
            var tile =
display.queue.getResult(levelGrid[x][y]);

            //Display the tile in the correct position
            var bitmap = new createjs.Bitmap(tile);
            bitmap.x = xPos;
            bitmap.y = yPos;
            display.stage.addChild(bitmap);

            //Position for next tile on the X-axis
            xPos += constant.TILEWIDTH;
        }

        //Position for the next tile on the Y-axis
        yPos += constant.TILEHEIGHT;
    }

}

function playGame()
{
    globals.playing = true;
    globals.gameTime = 0;
    displayScore();

}

function displayScore()
{
    display.stage.removeChild(globals.scoreText);
    globals.scoreText = new createjs.Text("Score: " +
globals.score , "30px Arial", "#ffffff");
    globals.scoreText.y = 10;
    globals.scoreText.x = 10;
    display.stage.addChild(globals.scoreText);
    display.stage.update();
}
```

```
function playLoop()
{

    if(globals.playing)
    {
        globals.gameTime = globals.gameTime + (1/15);

        if(globals.gameTime < constant.LEVELTIME)
        {
            //How Hard will the level be?
            if(globals.level == 1)
            {
                var frequency = constant.LEVEL1FREQUENCY;
            } else if (globals.level == 2)
            {
                var frequency =  constant.LEVEL2FREQUENCY;
            } else
            {
                var frequency = constant.LEVEL3FREQUENCY;
            }
            //If the numbers match-- create a mole
            var match = Math.floor((Math.random() *
frequency) + 0);
            if(match == 1)
            {
                createRandomMole();
            }
        } else

        {
            globals.playing = false;
            endLevel();
        }
    }
}

function createRandomMole()
{
```

```
    var numHoles = globals.holePositions.length/2;
    var where = Math.floor((Math.random() *
globals.holePositions.length) + 0);        //Where will the
mole appear?
            if(where % 2 != 0)
            {
                where--;
            }

            var y = globals.holePositions[where];
            var x = globals.holePositions[where+1];

            //Mole pops up
            display.popAnimation.x = x *
constant.TILEWIDTH;
            display.popAnimation.y = y *
constant.TILEHEIGHT;
            display.popAnimation.play();
            display.stage.addChild(display.popAnimation);
            display.stage.update();

            //Should the mole laugh at the player
            var playSound = Math.floor((Math.random() * 4)
+ 0);
            if (playSound ==3) {
createjs.Sound.play("snd_laugh"); }

            //After the mole pops up run a secondary
animation
            display.popAnimation.on("animationend",
function(){
                //which mole
                var which = Math.floor((Math.random() * 2)
+ 0);
                if(which == 0) { var mole =
display.laughingAnimation }
                else if (which ==1 ) {var mole =
display.idleAnimation }
                else {var mole = display.teaseAnimation };
```

```
                //display the mole in the proper location
display.stage.removeChild(display.popAnimation);
                mole.y = y * constant.TILEWIDTH;
                mole.x = x * constant.TILEWIDTH;
                mole.play();
                display.stage.addChild(mole);
                display.stage.update();
                mole.addEventListener("click", hit, false);
//What to do if the mole is "hit"
            });
}

function hit(mole)
{
    //Play a sound, and display the "hit" animation
    createjs.Sound.play("snd_punch");
    display.stage.removeChild(mole.target);
    globals.score = globals.score + 10;
    display.hitAnimation.x = mole.target.x;
    display.hitAnimation.y = mole.target.y;
    display.stage.addChild(display.hitAnimation);
    display.stage.update();
    displayScore();

    //When the animation is done, remove it
    display.hitAnimation.on("animationend", function(){
        display.stage.removeChild(display.hitAnimation);
    });
}


function endLevel()
{
    if(globals.level < 3)
    {
        globals.level++;
        loadLevel();
    } else
    {
```

```
            gameOver();
        }
    }

function gameOver()
{
    //Stop Sounds
    createjs.Sound.stop();

    //Remove Current Click Listener
    display.stage.removeAllEventListeners();

    //Display Level Screen
    display.stage.removeAllChildren();
    display.stage.update();

    var background =
display.queue.getResult("ls_gameOver");
    display.stage.addChild(new
createjs.Bitmap(background));
    display.stage.update();

    //Play welcome music
    createjs.Sound.play("snd_welcome");

    display.stage.addEventListener("click", function() {
        globals.level = 1;
        loadLevel();
        globals.score = 0;

    } );
}
```

Mise en Place – window.onload, init, setupCanvas, and preloadAssets

Mise en place is a French culinary term that means "putting in place", and refers to initially setting everything up so that you may begin doing what you've actually set out to do. The four functions that we're going to examine in this section all relate to that general idea – except in this case, the mise en place concept is applied to game programming rather than cooking.

Code Listing 8-1: window.onload

```
window.onload=function()
{
    init();
    //document.addEventListener('deviceready', init,
false);
}
```

The window.onload property stores the function that is called when index.html is loaded. It's essentially the starting point of our program. The only thing that happens in our window.onload function is a call to the init function. The line of code you see commented out is meant for use with Cordova/PhoneGap – we aren't using PhoneGap with our game, but you could by removing the two slashes and performing a few other steps. LearnToProgram has provided lessons on using PhoneGap, which is used to create native applications for various mobile devices. Feel free to explore those lessons if you're interested in making this game into a native mobile application.

Code Listing 8-2: init()

```
function init()
{
    setupCanvas();
    preloadAssets();
}
```

Our init function is also quite simple, as all it does is call two other functions – the setupCanvas function (which is used to setup our *canvas*) and the preloadAssets function (which is used to load the game assets). Let's take a look at each of those two functions.

Code Listing 8-3: setupCanvas()

```
function setupCanvas()
{
    display.stage = new createjs.Stage("myCanvas");
    display.stage.canvas.width = constant.WIDTH;
    display.stage.canvas.height = constant.HEIGHT;
}
```

The stage field of display is an *EaselJS* Stage object, which is used as the top level container for our game. It takes an HTML *canvas* element as an argument, which is used as the "stage" for our game. Then, we set the height and width of our *canvas* using the constant values defined in constants.js. If you want to change the height and width, just change the values in constants.js for constant.WIDTH and constant.HEIGHT. For more information on the *EaselJS* Stage class, view the documentation at http://createjs.com/docs/easeljs/classes/Stage.html

Code Listing 8-4: preloadAssets()

```
function preloadAssets()
{
    display.queue = new createjs.LoadQueue();
    display.queue.installPlugin(createjs.Sound);
    display.queue.on("complete" , assetsLoaded, this);
    display.queue.loadManifest([
```

```
        {id: "ls_title",
src:"assets/loadingScreens/ls_title.jpg"},
        {id: "ls_credit",
src:"assets/loadingScreens/ls_credit.jpg"},
        {id: "ls_gameOver",
src:"assets/loadingScreens/ls_gameOver.jpg"},
        {id: "ls_level1",
src:"assets/loadingScreens/ls_level1.jpg"},
        {id: "ls_level2",
src:"assets/loadingScreens/ls_level2.jpg"},
        {id: "ls_level3",
src:"assets/loadingScreens/ls_level3.jpg"},
        {id: "ls_winner",
src:"assets/loadingScreens/ls_winner.jpg"},
        {id: "bt_grass",
src:"assets/backgroundTiles/bt_grass.png"},
        {id: "bt_hole",
src:"assets/backgroundTiles/bt_hole.png"},
        {id: "bt_flowerRock",
src:"assets/backgroundTiles/bt_flowerRock.png"},
        {id: "bt_rock",
src:"assets/backgroundTiles/bt_rock.png"},
        {id: "bt_flowers",
src:"assets/backgroundTiles/bt_flowers.png"},
        {id: "snd_welcome",
src:"assets/sounds/welcome.mp3"},
        {id: "snd_punch", src:"assets/sounds/punch.mp3"},
        {id: "snd_level1Background",
src:"assets/sounds/circus1.mp3"},
        {id: "snd_level2Background",
src:"assets/sounds/circus2.mp3"},
        {id: "snd_level3Background",
src:"assets/sounds/circus3.mp3"},
        {id: "snd_laugh", src:"assets/sounds/laugh.mp3"},
        {id: "ss_hit",
src:"assets/spriteAnimations/spritesheet_hit.png"},
        {id: "ss_idle",
src:"assets/spriteAnimations/spritesheet_idle.png"},
        {id: "ss_laughing",
src:"assets/spriteAnimations/spritesheet_laughing.png"},
```

```
        {id: "ss_pop",
src:"assets/spriteAnimations/spritesheet_pop.png"},
        {id: "ss_tease",
src:"assets/spriteAnimations/spritesheet_tease.png"}

    ]);
}
```

Next, we call the preloadAssets() function, which is used to load all of our asset files. We start by creating a *PreloadJS* LoadQueue object, which we store in the queue property of our display Object (from display.js). The purpose of a LoadQueue object is to pre-load various files. In our case, we're preloading the various files in our assets folder - which is the images and sounds used in all of the output to our user. For more information on the *PreloadJS* LoadQueue class view the documentation at
http://www.createjs.com/docs/preloadjs/classes/LoadQueue.html

The installPlugin method of our LoadQueue object (display.queue) is used to install plugins. In this case, we're installing the *CreateJS* Sound plugin. This way, we can play the various sounds in our game (background music, sounds of the moles being wacked, etc). We use the on method of our LoadQueue Object to specify which function we should call when we're done loading all of our assets. Therefore, the on method essentially sets an event handler for the completion of our queue. We specify that the assetsLoaded method should be called once everything is loaded. In addition to setting an event listener for when everything is finished loading, you could also use the on method to set event listeners for errors, for when a single file finishes loading, or when any progress has been made in loading the files.

Finally, we use the loadManifest method of our LoadQueue object to actually load all of our files. As you can see, we also assign each of

```
```

these files an id, which we use in other parts of our source code. After loadManifest is finished loading our files, the control of our program is transferred to the assetsLoaded function, as we specified that method should be called after our assets are finished loading.

Welcoming the Player – assetsLoaded() and registerSpriteSheets()

After the preloadAssets function is finished, the assetsLoaded function is called:

Code Listing 9-1: assetsLoaded()

```
function assetsLoaded()
{
    //Display the Level1 Screen
    var background = display.queue.getResult("ls_title");
    display.stage.addChild(new
createjs.Bitmap(background));
    display.stage.update();

    //Reister Sprite Sheets
    registerSpriteSheets();

    //click to start the game
    display.stage.addEventListener("click", function(event)
{ loadLevel(); })

    //Play welcome music
    createjs.Sound.play("snd_welcome");
}
```

First, we store result from display.queue.getResult("ls_title") (which is
the id of our title screen image, as specified in loadManifest) in our
variable named background. This variable is then used to display the
image at assets/loadingScreens/ls_title.jpg (the file mapped to the id
ls_title, as shown in Figure 9-1) by passing our background variable as
an argument to the *EaselJS* Bitmap constructor. The Bitmap class is
used to create an *EaselJS* image, which we add to our stage via the
addChild function. Then, we call the update method of the Stage class
to actually display the image on our stage/canvas. For more information
on the *EaselJS* Bitmap class, view the official documentation at
http://createjs.com/docs/easeljs/classes/Bitmap.html

Figure 9-1 – ls_title.jpg

Next, we call the registerSpriteSheets() function, which is used to create our sprite animations. As mentioned earlier, a *sprite sheet* is an image that is actually made up of several images, or "frames", which get displayed in a sequence as an animation. We will explore the registerSpriteSheets() function in depth once we finish exploring the rest of our assetsLoaded() function.

After the registerSpriteSheets() function is finished, we create an event listener for click events, so that the loadLevel() function is called when the user clicks their mouse or taps their touchscreen. Until the user clicks, we also play background music (which is from the file associated with the id snd_welcome). This id is associated with the sound file assets/sounds/welcome.mp3, go ahead and play that file in an mp3 player. We use *SoundJS* (which is part of *CreateJS*) to take care of playing the sound. In particular, we use the play function of *SoundJS* to play the sound. Refer to the documentation listed earlier for *SoundJS* (in the *CreateJS* section of this document) for further information.

Now let's re-visit the registerSpriteSheets() function:

Code Listing 9-2: registerSpriteSheets()

```
function registerSpriteSheets()
{
    //Hit Spritesheet
    var data = {
        images: [display.queue.getResult("ss_hit")],
        frames: {width:170, height: 168},
        animations: { hit: [0,6] } , framerate: 10
    };

    var hitSpriteSheet = new createjs.SpriteSheet(data);
    display.hitAnimation = new
createjs.Sprite(hitSpriteSheet, "hit");

    //Idle Spritesheet
    var data = {
        images: [display.queue.getResult("ss_idle")],
        frames: {width:170, height: 168},
        animations: { idle: [0,6] } , framerate: 10
    };

    var idleSpriteSheet = new createjs.SpriteSheet(data);
    display.idleAnimation = new
createjs.Sprite(idleSpriteSheet, "idle");
```

```
    //Laughing Spritesheet
    var data = {
        images: [display.queue.getResult("ss_laughing")],
        frames: {width:170, height: 168},
        animations: { laugh: [0,12] } , framerate: 10
    };

    var laughingSpriteSheet = new
createjs.SpriteSheet(data);
    display.laughingAnimation = new
createjs.Sprite(laughingSpriteSheet, "laugh");

    //Pop Animation
    var data = {
        images: [display.queue.getResult("ss_pop")],
        frames: {width:170, height: 168},
        animations: { pop: [0,5] } , framerate: 10
    };

    var popSpriteSheet = new createjs.SpriteSheet(data);
    display.popAnimation = new
createjs.Sprite(popSpriteSheet, "pop");

    //Tease Animation
    var data = {
        images: [display.queue.getResult("ss_tease")],
        frames: {width:170, height: 168},
        animations: { tease: [0,13] } , framerate: 10
    };

    var teaseSpriteSheet = new createjs.SpriteSheet(data);
    display.teaseAnimation = new
createjs.Sprite(teaseSpriteSheet, "tease");

}
```

We register the *sprite sheet* via the *EaselJS* SpriteSheet class. The
constructor needs a few values, so we pass it values for the images, the

frames, and the animations. We store these values in our variable named data, and simply pass our data variable to the constructor.

The first parameter passed to our SpriteSheet constructor is the image that contains our *sprite sheet*. The second parameter specifies the height and width of each frame in the *sprite sheet*. The third parameter specifies which frames of the *sprite sheet* are used in our animation, as well as the frame rate. Let's look at the data passed to the constructor for our hit *sprite sheet* as an example:

Code Listing 9-3: The Hit Sprite Sheet

```
//Hit Spritesheet
    var data = {
        images: [display.queue.getResult("ss_hit")],
        frames: {width:170, height: 168},
        animations: { hit: [0,6] } , framerate: 10
    };
```

First, we specify that the *sprite sheet* for the animation played when we wack a mole is located in the image associated with the id "ss_hit". Next, we specify that the width and height of each frame is 170 x 168 pixels. Finally, animations: { hit: [0,6] } means we have 7 images that are used in the animation, and that we are using the frames from index 0 to index 6. We also specify that the frame rate for the animation is 10 frames per second.

We create our sprites by using the *EaselJS* Sprite class, which takes a SpriteSheet object as an argument. Essentially, all it does is create a sprite animation specified by the SpriteSheet passed to the constructor. As you can see, the sprites are stored in the various animation properties of our display object. For example, our hit sprite is stored in the display.hitAnimation property. This process is repeated for each of our sprite animations: the hit sprite, the idle sprite, the laughing sprite, the pop sprite, and the tease sprite. For more information on the *EaselJS* SpriteSheet and Sprite classes, refer to the official documentation at http://createjs.com/docs/easeljs/classes/SpriteSheet.html and http://createjs.com/docs/easeljs/classes/Sprite.html

Loading Each Level – loadLevel()

As soon as the user clicks, the loadLevel() function is called:

Code Listing 10-1: loadLevel()

```
function loadLevel()
{
    //Stop Sounds
    createjs.Sound.stop();

    //Remove Current Click Listener
    display.stage.removeAllEventListeners();

    //Display Level Screen
    display.stage.removeAllChildren();
    display.stage.update();

    var levelLabel = "ls_level" + globals.level;
    var level_screen = display.queue.getResult(levelLabel);
    display.stage.addChild(new
createjs.Bitmap(level_screen));
    display.stage.update();

    //Play Level Music
    var music = "snd_level" + globals.level + "Background";
    createjs.Sound.play(music,{loop:8});
```

```
    //Wait for click to start play
    display.stage.addEventListener("click", function(event)
{ startLevel(); })

}
```

First, we stop the currently playing sounds with createjs.Sound.stop(), which calls the *SoundJS* stop method. Second, we remove all of the current event listeners from the stage. The removeAllChildren removes all of the children from our stage (currently, that's just our background Bitmap). As we have seen before, the update method simply re-renders our stage.

Our levelLabel variable gets set to ls_levelX, where X is the value of globals.level. This is initially one, and each time we beat a level it increases by one. This way, the proper asset is loaded from display.queue in the next line of code. The next line of code creates a *CreateJS* bitmap from our level 1 image asset. Finally, we render it to our stage via the update function to display the start screen for our level.

We load the proper sound file for our level much like how we loaded the proper background image for our level - by using the global variable that holds our level to pick the proper asset. The last line of code in loadLevel() creates an event listener for click events so that we call the startLevel() function (which starts the level) when the user clicks.

Starting the Level – startLevel(), createLevelGrid(), and displayLevelGrid()

Once the user clicks again, then the startLevel function is called.

Code Listing 11-1: startLevel()

```
function startLevel()
{
    //Remove Level Screen
    display.stage.removeAllChildren();
    display.stage.removeAllEventListeners();

    //Display the Level Grid
    var levelGrid = createLevelGrid(constant.COLUMNS,
constant.ROWS);
    displayLevelGrid(levelGrid, constant.COLUMNS,
constant.ROWS);

    //Make a simple array of hole positions
    globals.holePositions = new Array();
    for(x=0; x < levelGrid.length; x++)
    {
        for(y=0; y < levelGrid[x].length; y++)
        {
            if(levelGrid[x][y] == "bt_hole")
            {
                globals.holePositions.push(x);
                globals.holePositions.push(y);
            }
        }
    }

    //start ticker
```

```
    createjs.Ticker.setFPS(15);
    createjs.Ticker.addEventListener('tick',
display.stage);
    createjs.Ticker.addEventListener('tick', playLoop);

    playGame();
}
```

First, we remove the loading screen of the level with the
removeAllChildren() method, and also remove the click event listener
with the removeAllEventListeners() method. Second, we create the
level grid and then display the level grid using the createLevelGrid and
displayLevelGrid functions. Let's examine each of those functions in
depth right now, since they are necessary for understanding the rest of
the startLevel() function.

Code Listing 11-2: createLevelGrid(colsNumber, rowsNumber)

```
function createLevelGrid(colsNumber, rowsNumber)
{
    var levelGrid= new Array();

    //Each Row
    for(var x=0; x < rowsNumber; x++)
        {
            var row = new Array();
            //Each column in that row
            for(var y = 0; y < colsNumber; y++)
             {
                var tileType = Math.floor((Math.random() *
4) + 0);

                //Associate Graphic with numerical tileType
                if(tileType ==0)
                {
                    tileType = "bt_grass";
                } else if (tileType ==1)
                {
```

```
                tileType = "bt_hole";
         } else if (tileType ==2)
         {
                tileType = "bt_flowerRock";
         } else if (tileType ==3)
         {
                tileType = "bt_rock";
         } else
         {
                tileType = "bt_flowers";
         }
         row[y] = tileType;
      }
      levelGrid[x] = row;
   }
   return levelGrid;
}
```

The createLevelGrid(colsNumber, rowsNumber) function has two
parameters. The first parameter (colsNumber) represents the number of
columns for our grid. The second parameter (rowsNumber) represents
the number of rows for our grid. In startLevel(), the arguments passed
to createLevelGrid are the constant values we declared in constant.js
for our columns and rows. We create an array named levelGrid, which
is actually a 2 dimensional array (one dimension for the rows, and
another dimension for the columns). We use two for loops (one nested
inside the other) to fill the array. Each iteration of the outer for loop
creates a row, and the inner for loop fills each field of that row with a
tile. We use the Math.random() function to choose a random number
between 0 and 4, which determines which tile to use to fill that
particular field of the row (as you can see in the if statements). The
levelGrid array is actually returned from this function, which is stored
in the levelGrid variable in our startLevel() function.

After the createLevelGrid(colsNumber, rowsNumber) function is finished executing, the flow of the program goes back to our startLevel() function. The next line of code in startLevel() calls the displayLevelGrid function. Let's take a look at that function:

Code Listing 11-3: displayLevelGrid(levelGrid, colsNumber, rowsNumber)

```
function displayLevelGrid(levelGrid, colsNumber,
rowsNumber)
{
    //Where will the tile be positioned?
    var xPos=0;
    var yPos=0;

    for(var x = 0; x < rowsNumber; x++)
    {
        xPos = 0;
        for(var y =0; y < colsNumber; y++)
        {
            var tile =
display.queue.getResult(levelGrid[x][y]);

            //Display the tile in the correct position
            var bitmap = new createjs.Bitmap(tile);
            bitmap.x = xPos;
            bitmap.y = yPos;
            display.stage.addChild(bitmap);

            //Position for next tile on the X-axis
            xPos += constant.TILEWIDTH;
        }

        //Position for the next tile on the Y-axis
        yPos += constant.TILEHEIGHT;
    }
```

}

The displayLevelGrid function has three parameters: levelGrid, colsNumber, and rowsNumber. In startLevel(), the arguments we pass to the displayLevelGrid function is the levelGrid array (created by the createLevelGrid function), our columns constant, and our rows constant.

We use a nested for loop much like in createLevelGrid to create and display each tile. Each tile is actually a *EaselJS* Bitmap object. We set the x and y position of each tile with the xPos and yPos variables, which start at 0 and then increment with each iteration based on the TILEWIDTH and TILEHEIGHT constants declared in constant.js. We also add each tile to our stage by using the addChild method of the *EaselJS* Stage class. Once the displayLevelGrid function is finished, control is transferred back to the startLevel function.

Back in the startLevel function, we fill the array of the hole positions for the moles to come out of. Once again, we use nested for loops to accomplish this, much like in createLevelGrid and displayLevelGrid. We check every single value in levelGrid - each iteration of the inner for loop is a specific x,y index in levelGrid. If the tile value is "bt_hole", this means that it is a mole hole tile. In this case, we "push" the x and y values of that tile into our holePositions property of our globals object (which is from globals.js). The push method simply adds a value to the end of an array.

Finally, we use the *EaselJS* Ticker class to start our "ticker" and also set the FPS rate of it. Essentially, our ticker goes off after a specific time interval; in this case, 15 times per second. We add two event listeners for our tick event, so each time it ticks (every 1/15 of a second) our *EaselJS* Stage object responds and our playLoop function is called. The last line of code in startLevel() calls the playGame() function.

Starting the Gameplay - playGame() and displayScore()

Before we examine the playLoop function (which is essentially our main game loop), let's look at the function called in the last line of code in our startLevel function, as shown in Code Listing 12-1:

Code Listing 12-1: playGame()

```
function playGame()
{
    globals.playing = true;
    globals.gameTime = 0;
    displayScore();
}
```

The playGame function is quite simple. First, it sets our global variable playing to true, which means that the game is currently active. This needs to be set to true for the playLoop function to do anything, which we will look at later. It also sets our global gameTime variable to zero, so that we essentially reset the clock at the start of each level. Finally, the displayScore() method is called, as shown in Code Listing 12-2:

Code Listing 12-2: displayScore()

```
function displayScore()
{
    display.stage.removeChild(globals.scoreText);
    globals.scoreText = new createjs.Text("Score: " +
globals.score , "30px Arial", "#ffffff");
    globals.scoreText.y = 10;
    globals.scoreText.x = 10;
    display.stage.addChild(globals.scoreText);
    display.stage.update();
}
```

The displayScore method is also quite simple. It first removes the existing score with display.stage.removeChild(globals.scoreText). Then, we create an *EaselJS* Text object for displaying the score. We pass 3 arguments to the *EaselJS* Text class constructor - the first is the text we want to display, the second is the font size and type, and the third argument is the font color. Finally, we set the coordinates (x and y position) for the text and add it to our stage. We also call the update function to render our score (the *EaselJS* Text object) as shown in Figure 12-1 (the score is outlined in red):

Figure 12-1: The Score

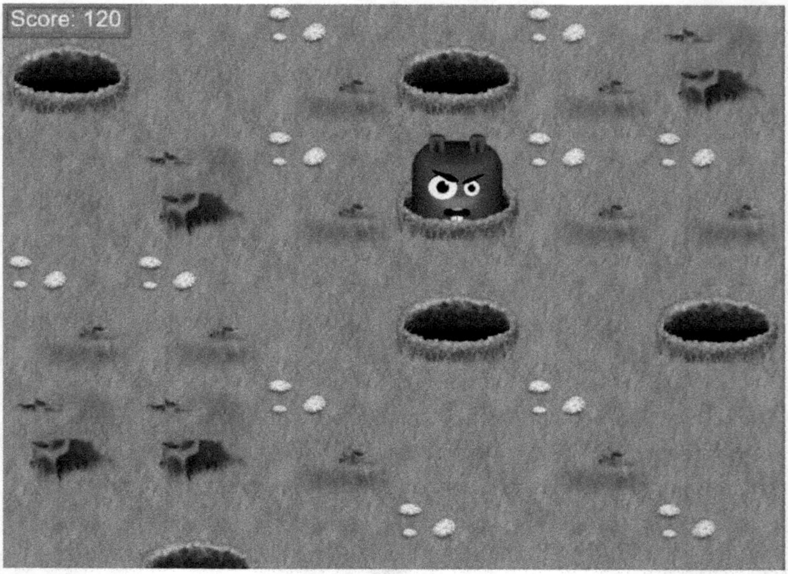

Figure 12-1: The Score

The Game Loop – playLoop() and endLevel()

Now let's look at the playLoop function, as shown in Code Listing 13-1:

Code Listing 13-1: playLoop()

```
function playLoop()
{

    if(globals.playing)
    {
```

```
        globals.gameTime = globals.gameTime + (1/15);

        if(globals.gameTime < constant.LEVELTIME)
        {
            //How Hard will the level be?
            if(globals.level == 1)
            {
                var frequency = constant.LEVEL1FREQUENCY;
            } else if (globals.level == 2)
            {
                var frequency =  constant.LEVEL2FREQUENCY;
            } else
            {
                var frequency = constant.LEVEL3FREQUENCY;
            }
            //If the numbers match-- create a mole
            var match = Math.floor((Math.random() *
frequency) + 0);
            if(match == 1)
            {
                createRandomMole();
            }

        } else

        {
            globals.playing = false;
            endLevel();
        }
    }
}
```

First we check if global.playing is set to true, since this value identifies whether or not we're actively playing the game. If the playing property is false, then playLoop() simply exits and the program's flow of execution returns to the function that called playLoop.() If globals.playing is true, then we increment our game time variable by

1/15 - the reason for this is because we are playing at 15 ticks per second (meaning playLoop gets called 15 times per second). We also have another conditional statement that checks if the current game time is less than the LEVELTIME constant we defined in constants.js. This constant specifies how many seconds each level goes on for (in our case, we have defined it to be 20, but you could change the value if you want to).

Next, we check the value of globals.level (which specifies which level we are on) to set the value of a variable named frequency. The value of frequency is dependent upon which level we are on. We assign it the constant value specified in constants.js associated with the level specified by globals.level. Finally, we use a random number generator function (Math.random) to potentially create a random mole. The lower the value of frequency, the more often a mole will be created, since it is created whenever our random value (stored in the variable match) is one. We will take a look at the createRandomMole() function later - for now, just know that it causes a mole to pop out of a random hole. Once we run out of time in the level, the code in the else block executes, which sets globals.playing to false and ends the level (via the endLevel() function).

Before we take a look at the createRandomMole() function, let's examine the end level function, as shown in Code Listing 13-2:

Code Listing 13-2: endLevel()

```
function endLevel()
{
    if(globals.level < 3)
    {
```

62

```
        globals.level++;
        loadLevel();
    } else
    {
        gameOver();
    }
}
```

The endLevel function first checks if the current level is less than 3. Since there are 3 levels in the game, if we haven't beaten the third level yet, we increment the value of globals.level (our global variable which keeps track of the current level). Then, we call the loadLevel() function to load the new level. On the other hand, if we just finished the third level (which means globals.level is not less than three), the else block executes, which calls the gameOver() function.

Popping Up Moles – createRandomMole()

Before we look at the gameOver() function, let's take a look at the createRandomMole() function, as shown in Code Listing 14-1:

Code Listing 14-1: createRandomMole()

```
function createRandomMole()
{
    var numHoles = globals.holePositions.length/2;
    var where = Math.floor((Math.random() *
globals.holePositions.length) + 0);    //Where will the
mole appear?
```

```
if(where % 2 != 0)
{
    where--;
}

var y = globals.holePositions[where];
var x = globals.holePositions[where+1];

//Mole pops up
display.popAnimation.x = x *
constant.TILEWIDTH;
display.popAnimation.y = y *
constant.TILEHEIGHT;
display.popAnimation.play();
display.stage.addChild(display.popAnimation);
display.stage.update();

//Should the mole laugh at the player
var playSound = Math.floor((Math.random() * 4)
+ 0);
if (playSound ==3) {
createjs.Sound.play("snd_laugh"); }

//After the mole pops up run a secondary
animation
display.popAnimation.on("animationend",
function(){
    //which mole
    var which = Math.floor((Math.random() * 2)
+ 0);
    if(which == 0) { var mole =
display.laughingAnimation }
    else if (which ==1 ) {var mole =
display.idleAnimation }
    else {var mole = display.teaseAnimation };

    //display the mole in the proper location

display.stage.removeChild(display.popAnimation);
    mole.y = y * constant.TILEWIDTH;
```

```
            mole.x = x * constant.TILEWIDTH;
            mole.play();
            display.stage.addChild(mole);
            display.stage.update();
            mole.addEventListener("click", hit, false);
//What to do if the mole is "hit"
        });
}
```

First, we determine the number of holes by dividing our
globals.holePositions property by two. The reason we divide by two is
because there are values in holePositions for each x value and each y
value of the hole positions. Since there are two separate values (one x
and one y) for each position, we must divide by two. The where
variable stores a randomly generated value for determining where the
mole should appear - the reason we're using a random number
generator is because we want the moles to appear at random, rather
than follow any noticeable pattern. Technically, random number
generators generally follow some sort of pattern, but they at least
appear to be random. We also make sure that the value in where is
divisible by 2 (divisible by 2 means that it's an even number), since y
values are at even indexes in holePositions and y values are at odd
indexes in holePositions. If where is not an even number, we subtract
one from it to transform it into an odd number. This is so that where
can be equivalent to a y value (an even index in holePositions), and
where + 1 can be equivalent to a x value (an odd index in
holePositions). We then set the x and y values for the mole accordingly,
storing holePositions[where] in y and holePositions[where + 1] in x.

The next lines of code use our popAnimation sprite (originally declared
in display.js, and initialized in registerSpriteSheets()) to play the
animation for a mole popping up. We also add the sprite to our stage,
and call the update function to render the animation. As you can see,

```
```

the random function is a recurring theme - random number generators are very useful in game programming, since much game programming is meant to produce spontaneity. As a side note, the Math.floor function removes anything after the decimal place of the value passed to it. That way, we are dealing with integers rather than decimal values (integers are easier to work with for certain things). Also, we multiply the result of Math.random() by however high we want our value to potentially be, since the random function creates a value between zero (inclusive) and one (exclusive). Therefore, by multiplying it by 4 and flooring it, we generate either a zero, a one, a two, or a three (four possible values). If the value returned is three, the mole laughs at the player. Hence, there's a 25% chance that the mole will laugh at you when it pops out of the hole.

We use *SoundJS* to play the laughing sound just like we have used it to play other sounds. The last thing that we do in createRandomMole is add an event listener for our animationend event of our popAnimation sprite. As you may have already guessed, the "animationend" event is fired after the popup animation is complete. When the event handler is activated, we use a random number generator (once again) to determine whether we should play the idle animation, the laughing animation, or the tease animation. Next, we remove the popup animation from our stage. Finally, we use mole.play(), stage.addChild(), and stage.update() to play the animation stored in our mole variable, add it to our stage, and render our updated stage to the screen. Before completely exiting the block of code for our event handler, we create a click event handler for our mole, since clicking on the mole means the mole is wacked (or hit). When triggered, this event handler calls the hit(mole) function.

Wacking the Mole – hit(mole)

When a mole is wacked, the hit function is called. The code for the hit function is shown in Code Listing 15-1:

Code Listing 15-1: hit(mole)

```
function hit(mole)
{
    //Play a sound, and display the "hit" animation
    createjs.Sound.play("snd_punch");
    display.stage.removeChild(mole.target);
    globals.score = globals.score + 10;
    display.hitAnimation.x = mole.target.x;
    display.hitAnimation.y = mole.target.y;
    display.stage.addChild(display.hitAnimation);
    display.stage.update();
    displayScore();

    //When the animation is done, remove it
    display.hitAnimation.on("animationend", function(){
        display.stage.removeChild(display.hitAnimation);
    });
}
```

First, this function uses the play method of *SoundJS* to play the punch sound. We remove the animation for the mole that was hit via display.stage.removeChild(mole.target), and replace that animation with the hit animation. The target property is used to specify that we are referring to the mole that was clicked. The x and y values that determine which tile should play the hit animation are based on the x and y values of the click (specified by mole.target.x, and mole.target.y). Next, we increase the score (stored in globals.score) by 10, to reward the player for wacking the mole. Then, we call the update function to render everything and display the score via the displayScore function (which we covered earlier). At the end of our hit function, we create an event handler for when the hit animation is done playing. The only thing this event handler does is remove the hit animation sprite from our stage. The frames of the hit animation are shown in Figure 15-1:

Figure 15-1: The Hit Sprite Sheet

Ending the Game – gameOver()

At this point, the only function we have not covered is the gameOver() function. The source code for our gameOver function is shown in Code Listing 16-1:

Code Listing 16-1: gameOver()

```
function gameOver()
{
    //Stop Sounds
    createjs.Sound.stop();

    //Remove Current Click Listener
    display.stage.removeAllEventListeners();

    //Display Level Screen
    display.stage.removeAllChildren();
    display.stage.update();
```

```
    var background =
display.queue.getResult("ls_gameOver");
    display.stage.addChild(new
createjs.Bitmap(background));
    display.stage.update();

    //Play welcome music
    createjs.Sound.play("snd_welcome");

    display.stage.addEventListener("click", function() {
        globals.level = 1;
        loadLevel();
        globals.score = 0;

    } );
}
```

As the name implies, this function ends the game. We stop all the
sounds using the *SoundJS* stop function, we remove all the event
listeners for our stage, and we remove all children (objects) from our
stage. Then, we display the game over image on our stage (as shown in
Figure 16-1), and play the welcome music (once again, using *SoundJS*).

Figure 16-1: The Game Over Screen

However, the game isn't necessarily over – since before exiting the gameOver() function, we create a click event listener that restarts the game when triggered (by setting the level to 1, setting the score to 0, and calling the loadLevel() function). So all you need to do is click, and a new game begins. This way, the player is more likely to continue to waste time playing our game, and it can keep going on forever. There are always more moles to wack!

Online Courses from LearnToProgram

Become a Certified Web Developer Level One

Become a Certified Web Developer Level Two

Certified Mobile Developer

Roadmap to Web Developer

HTML and CSS for Beginners (with HTML5

Javascript for Beginners

Programming for Absolute Beginners

PHP and MySQL for Beginners

jQuery for Beginners

CSS Development with CSS3

Node.js for Beginners

Advanced Javascript Development

AJAX Development

SQL Database for Beginners

Ruby on Rails for Beginners

Famo.us Javascript Framework

GitHub Fundamentals

Creating a PHP Login Script

Front End Developer with Adobe Dreamweaver

Codeless Web Development with Adobe Muse

Mobile App Development with HTML5

10 Apps in 10 Weeks

Java Programming for Beginners

Swift Language Fundamentals

iOS Development for Beginners

Android Development for Beginners

10 Apps in 10 Weeks:iOS Edition

Python for Beginners

Construct 2 for Beginners

Game Development with Unity

Mobile Game Development for iOS

3D Fundamentals with iOS

Project Management using Microsoft Project

.Net for Beginners

C++ for Beginners

Joomla for Beginners

User Experience Design Fundamentals

Photoshop CS6 Training for Coders

Design for Coders

C Programming for Beginners

Objective C for Beginners

Introduction to Web Development

Game Development Fundamentals with Python

www.ingramcontent.com/pod-product-compliance
Lightning Source LLC
Chambersburg PA
CBHW061031050326
40689CB00012B/2767